Sunshine
– Rays of Hope

Dhwani Sangani

BookLeaf
Publishing

India | USA | UK

Presentation by *BookLeaf Publishing*

Web: www.bookleafpub.com

E-mail: info@bookleafpub.com

ISBN: 9789363318830

First edition 2024

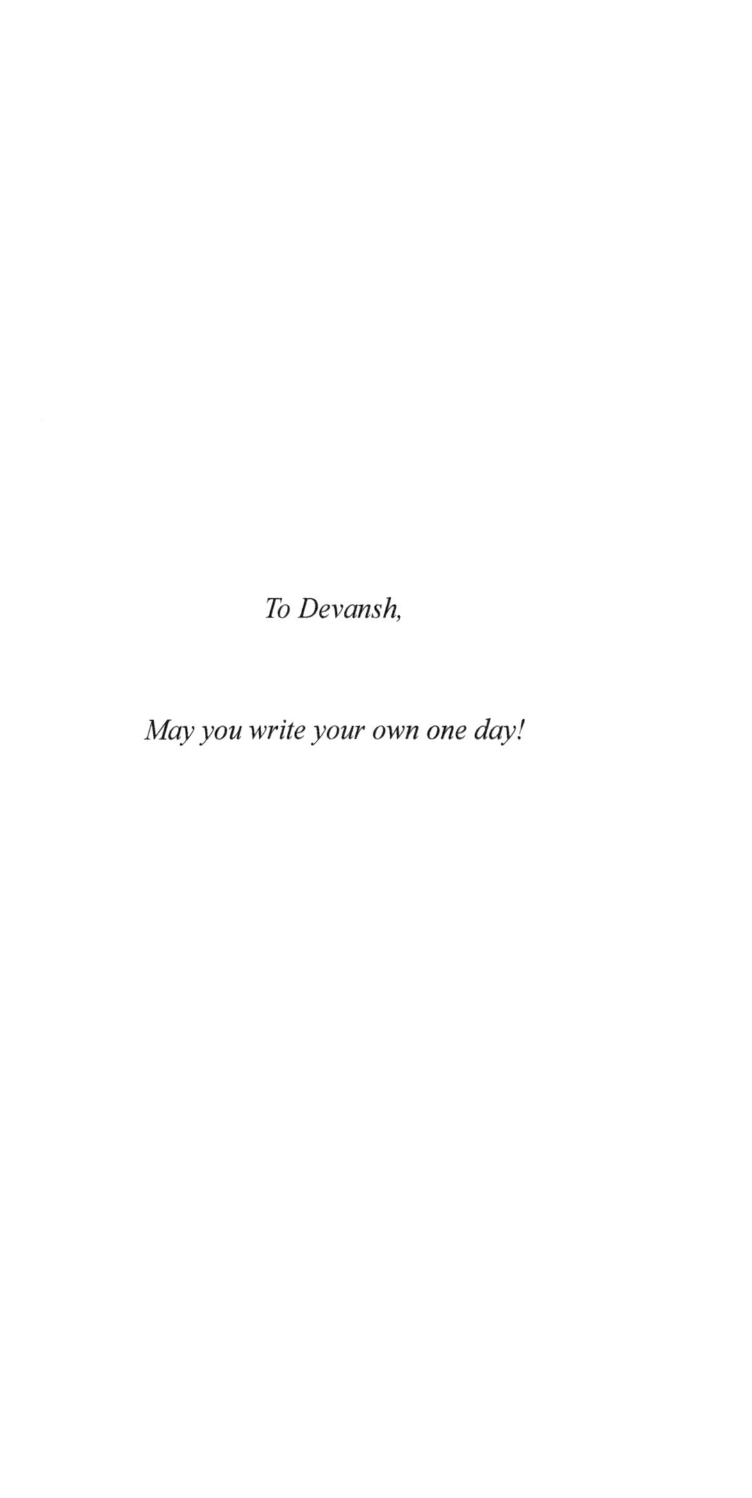

To Devansh,

May you write your own one day!

ACKNOWLEDGEMENTS

Creating this collection has been a journey of introspection, creativity and growth, and it would not have been possible without the support and encouragement of many wonderful people.

First and foremost, I would like to thank my family – My Four Parents; My Husband, Pratik; my Brother Sahil & my lifeline (my son), Devansh – for their unwavering love and belief in me. Your constant support has been my greatest source of strength.

To my readers, thank you for embarking on this journey with me. Your interest and support gave life to these poems and made this endeavour truly meaningful.

Lastly, to everyone who has ever shared their stories with me, whether in passing conversations or deep exchanges, thank you. Your experiences have enriched my understanding of life and have found a place within these pages.

With gratitude,

Dhwani

PREFACE

Life is a mosaic of moments, each with its own story to tell. In this collection, I have sought to capture the essence of these moments through the art of poetry. Each poem in this book is a reflection of the diverse experiences that shape our existence, from the quiet whispers of our innermost thoughts to the roaring tides of our greatest passions.

As you journey through these pages, you will encounter stories of love and loss, joy and sorrow, hope and despair. These poems are born from my own observations and experiences, but they also belong to anyone who has ever felt the weight of the world or the lightness of a fleeting moment.

Poetry has the power to distil complex emotions into a few carefully chosen words, to transform the mundane into the extraordinary. My hope is that within these verses, you will find echoes of your own life, your own struggles and your own triumphs. May these poems inspire you to look more closely at the world around you and to cherish the beauty in every aspect of life.

Thank you for allowing me to share these stories
with you. It is my sincerest wish that they
resonate with you and bring a sense of
connection and understanding.

With gratitude,
Dhwani

Then & Now!

Her hands were all sweaty,
nervousness evident to those who knew.
But the moment she started speaking,
the entire crowd fell silent.
Something was amiss,
something was not right.
She was there, yet it felt
like she was not supposed to be.
Yet she continued her music
as if she were alone in the room,
just like her 12-year-old self,
singing in front of the mirror,
tapping her foot slowly
while her hands performed a solo
dance of their own.
And soon it evaporated–

the fear, the anguish, the dilemma,
the anxiety, the doubts, the confusions.
People were enthralled by her act.
What more could a 90-year-old wish for?
What more could a dreamy teenager wish for...

Pain – Boon or Bane!

Sometimes it takes me days,

sometimes even months,

to escape the wilderness of nature

and get back to this holy sanctity of words.

Motivation, inspiration and ideas

don't exist when I am happy.

Why is it so?

Pain brings out the best in me.

Pain takes me to places I've never been.

Pain is the trigger for my writing,

and trust me, my friend,

pain is inevitable, just like death...

Good to your Bad

Be a slave to your habits.

Be a demon to your fears.

Be a hurricane to your worries.

Be good to your bad.

Yet

When you are in chaos, yet

you choose to feel energised,

accept the world as it is,

and find happiness in the imperfections,

because you just don't know–

life may stop existing tomorrow.

But the memories you made,

the happiness you felt,

the tears you cried,

the pain you endured,

the choices you made,

will stay for a lifetime...

Acceptance

We take an eternity to accept ourselves, or sometimes we even don't.

Then, why do we throw tantrums in accepting others?

Everybody is different, and life would be boring if they were a carbon copy of you.

So, why bother wasting time being sad or vulnerable!

Accept yourself first and then eventually

you'll find accepting others

the way they are – comparatively easy...

To Do or Not!

Life is to figure out

when to speak your mind

and when to let your calm rule...

Hard!

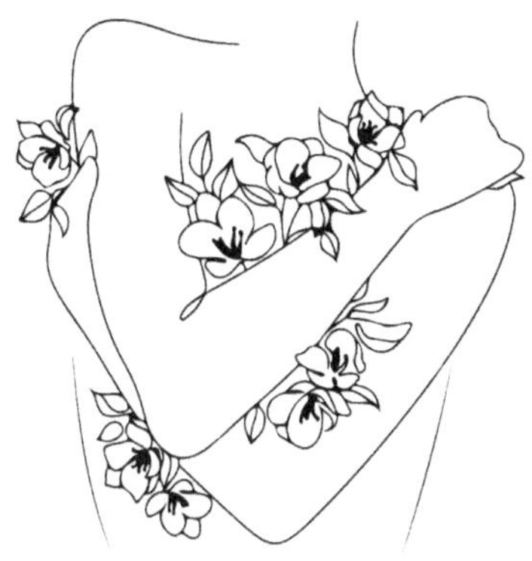

People will prick you all the time;

decide who's worth it.

People will tell you things are hard;

try it for yourself and prove your worth.

People will leave you when you need them the most;

let them go, and you'll grow stronger at your worst.

People will misguide you on your journey;

stay firm in your roots with peace and
harmony...

Alone

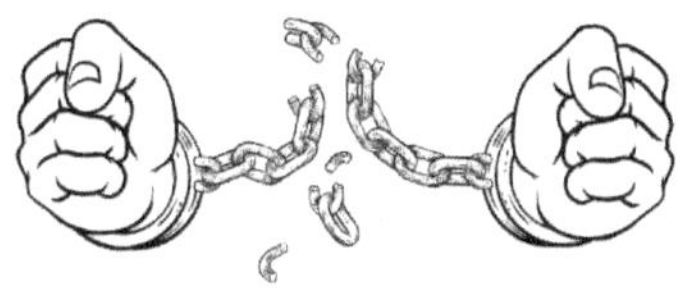

Alone were the thoughts, so was I.

Options were many; I had to pry.

Choosing was difficult–

Sad Happy or Happy Sad.

Lastly, the most powerful of them won the game.

Tell me yours; please give it a name!

Love is

Love is not only in saying, 'I love you'.

It's in being there when they tell you not to.

It's in doing things you don't like for them.

It's in sharing your favourite food with them.

It's loving without even asking for it.

Your childhood is over when…

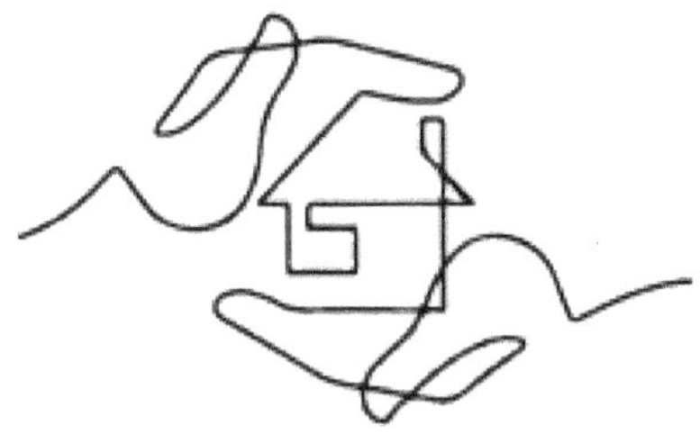

When you know your little tears won't make the wall collapse.

When you know your little fears won't bring a big hug.

When you know your little desires are neglected.

When you know you are not on the priority list.

When you know crying aloud won't bring solace.

When mom is not the answer to all problems.

When dad is not there to protect you from the outside world.

When you no longer fight with your brother for the TV remote control.

Let's ignite that lost innocence,

Let's be trusted again,

Let's be a child again and bring our childhood back...

Chase

Not everything,

not everyone,

requires chasing.

Things that are meant to be,

people who are meant to be,

will never make you feel territorial.

They'll just be there, somewhere in some corner,

silently supporting you,

cheering you,

loving you and caring for you.

The real challenge is to figure out:

Who the hell are they?

This, That & What Not!

Connecting the dots,

this, that and what not.

Sounds of laughter win the race;

unnoticed go those gasps of pain.

Life is good; life is a show–

the merrier the photo,

the brighter you grow.

But only if seen inside out:

the washroom holds more stories

than any social media account...

Hesitate!

It takes

a single step

to cross

those tons of hurdles,

fictional and imaginary,

running through our minds,

yet we hesitate...

Kuch Alfaz

Vo phir se un betuke sawalon mein ulajh gae,

'Tum mere ho ya Main tumhari'...

'She'Ro

She saw her reflection in the mirror.

It manifested all her flaws,

her grave life lessons,

her hard-earned respect,

her entire life slipping by.

Nothing was in her control

except for making that person

staring back at her happy.

MAD

MAD people are stared at,

pointed out,

But hell, do they care?

They carry on,

they persist until their MADNESS

turns into SUCCESS,

and they win, they conquer the world.

They do things that sane people

never dreamed of...

Lullaby

His heartbeat served as a lullaby,

taking her away from her horrific past...

Luxury!

♥She desired all those luxuries,

a happy heart could wish for.

but when love came knocking,

she settled, letting in every ounce,

a contented heart could yearn for♥

Home

her eyes had that magnetic effect on him,

he was naturally drawn towards those

crystalline – a labyrinth of emotions,

with a myriad of thoughts,

searching for something called 'Home'

Beautiful

She is beautiful with her scars,

She is beautiful with her broken heart,

She is beautiful with her daunting experiences,

She is beautiful with her dark past,

She is beautiful because she stands strong,

She is beautiful because she is independent,

She is beautiful because she learned her lessons
the hard way,

She is beautiful because she can take care of
herself,

She is beautiful; that's what she believes,

She is beautiful because she made herself so!

Kuch Alfaz

Khud hi ko kar buland itna, Aandhi bhi takrae to usse bhi maza aa jae...

www.ingramcontent.com/pod-product-compliance
Lightning Source LLC
Chambersburg PA
CBHW071235140726
47996CB00007B/2609